Ethics and the Arms Trade

Philip Towle

Published by the IEA Trade and Development Unit, 1998

First published in July 1998 by
The Trade and Development Unit
The Institute of Economic Affairs
2 Lord North Street
Westminster
London SW1P 3LB

IEA Studies in Trade and Development No. 1
All rights reserved
ISBN 0-255 36465-2

Many IEA publications are translated into languages other than English or are reprinted. Permission to translate or to reprint should be sought from the General Director at the address above.

Printed in Great Britain by
Hartington Fine Arts Limited, Lancing, West Sussex
Set in Times New Roman and Univers

Contents

Foreword *Gerald Frost*	5
The Author	8
Introduction	9
The Past	9
The End of the Cold War	12
The Impact on Arms Manufacturing	15
The Nature of Conflict After the Cold War	17
Arms Sales and Government Repression	19
Arms Sales and Inter-State Conflicts	21
Arms Sales and Casualties	24
Arms Deals and Third World Resources	25
The Response from Defence Industries	27
Conclusion	29
Summary	*Back Cover*

Table 1:	
Defence Expenditure in Constant 1995 US Dollars (million)	14
Defence Expenditure Per Capita in US Dollars	14
Percentage of GDP Spent on Defence	14
Table 2:	
Arms Imports in Constant 1995 US Dollars (million)	16

Foreword

Among the election promises of the Labour Government elected in May 1997 was a pledge to pursue a more 'ethical' foreign policy. As Mr Robin Cook, the Foreign Secretary, had already made plain, one prominent feature of this policy would be a more discriminating – and by implication, more restrictive – approach to the foreign sales of defence equipment by British companies. Accordingly, the system of export licensing in respect of arms sales would be made more 'transparent and accountable'.

In line with the new policy Mr Cook promptly vetoed the export of six Land Rovers to Indonesia and, taking advantage of Britain's presidency of the European Union, set about building support among Britain's EU partners for common guidelines governing the sales of defence equipment. The purpose of the guidelines, upon which agreement was reached in May 1998, was to prevent EU states from exploiting restraint by other members. They have been widely criticised, however, on the grounds that they merely require governments to explain themselves when granting licences in respect of orders previously denied by EU partners. The critics, including spokesmen for other EU countries, members of Mr Cook's own parliamentary party, and a range of non-governmental organisations, point out that there is nothing to prevent EU states reaching quite different conclusions when interpreting the common criteria by which licence applications are to be judged.

Domestic critics of Mr Cook's approach also appear unhappy that so far the proportion of export licence applications turned down by the Labour Government is no greater than that under the last Conservative Government. (The defence industry may complain that several orders appear to have been lost as a result of the new policy but this has been because of the delays to which it has led.)

In the circumstances, it seems unlikely that Mr Cook has yet fully satisfied those who share his enthusiasm for an 'ethical' approach to arms sales; and it is probable that the pressure on him to go further will continue. But, argues Dr Philip Towle, the author of this study – the first to be published by the IEA's Trade and Development Unit – additional steps to restrict the sale of arms to overseas customers could have consequences that go beyond the further shrinkage of an industry which has become even more important with the contraction of Britain's own armed forces. Such measures could undermine British defence preparedness, restrict the development of the nation's technological base, limit the effectiveness of British foreign policy while at the same time encouraging the development of indigenous arms production in the Third World. In his view, the danger is that a predominantly emotional response could weaken Britain's ability to deal with future security threats while doing nothing to help regions driven by conflict.

The rationale for a more 'ethical' approach to the sale of defence equipment thus requires careful scrutiny. In examining that rationale Dr Towle identifies a number of questionable assumptions. These include the assertion that arms sales assist repressive states in perpetrating human rights abuses and even in carrying out campaigns of genocide; that they cause war; that they increase the number of casualties in war situations; and that they prevent economic development in poor countries that would be better off spending scarce resources on infrastructure rather than on weapons.

Dr Towle finds weaknesses in all of these arguments. Repressive states do not need expensive modern weaponry to abuse or slaughter their citizens: the worst acts of genocide have involved small arms or extremely primitive weapons. Wars are the result of political conflicts, not 'arms races': the latter may serve as barometers of conflict, and even determine the moment when wars occur, but they do not cause them. There is no evidence to suggest a correlation between the level of arms expenditure and the level of casualties: arms sales to Sub-Saharan Africa have fallen during the last decade, one of the bloodiest in its history. And while arms expenditure may direct investment away from productive uses, it has not prevented economic development: Taiwan is just one example of a state that has enjoyed rapid economic expansion while spending heavily on defence.

Dr Towle accepts, however, that on balance there may be grounds for a ban on the exports of small arms. Small arms can be used for purposes of oppression, and in so far as a ban would restrict the numbers of such weapons falling into the hands of criminal organisations in the West, would coincide with self-interest. In his view, it would also help reduce the confusion between different types of weapons and their impact that he believes is responsible for some criticism of the defence industry.

The extent of that confusion makes it all the more necessary to bear in mind that, as during the Cold War, weapons can be used to deter aggression and to repair imbalances of military power, as well as to initiate conflict and to endanger stability. It is also important frankly to acknowledge the fact that order is a necessary condition of economic advance and the emergence of civil society. Before condemning Third World leaders for failing to meet Western standards of civil liberty and consequently denying them the means to maintain power, we need to be very sure that their successors will represent an improvement; otherwise we will be guilty of putting the purity of our motives before the interests of those we seek to help. Such a failure in understanding would surely vitiate any attempt to place foreign policy on more ethical foundations.

As with all Institute publications, the views expressed in this paper are those of the author, not of the Institute (which has no corporate view), its Trustees, Advisers or Directors. Nevertheless, we are indebted to Dr Towle for a lucid and thoughtful treatment of a topical and important subject.

June 1998 GERALD FROST
Director, IEA Trade and Development Unit

The Author

The author is the Director of the Centre of International Studies at Cambridge University. He has previously worked for the Foreign and Commonwealth Office, for the Australian National University in Canberra and for Reuters News Agency. He has written widely, particularly on arms control and on East Asian affairs. His most recent book on *Enforced Disarmament* was published by Clarendon Press in 1987. He is now editing a collection of essays on the treatment of prisoners of war in Asia during the Second World War and completing a book on post-war peace-making.

Introduction

The British defence manufacturing industry is facing greater problems and a more uncertain future than at any time since the 1920s. Sales at home have fallen dramatically, plants have closed and more than 300,000 jobs have been lost since 1980, 160,000 during the last decade. Yet the industry in Britain and elsewhere is still a major employer. It is also a safeguard against a very uncertain future. No New World Order has materialised, the former colonial empires will remain unstable for decades to come, ethnic rivalries in the Caucasus, the Balkans and parts of Africa have intensified and the possibility is ever present of a major new security threat emerging from a state equipped with weapons of mass destruction. The industry may now face new problems arising from the attempt to create a more 'moral' approach to arms sales and the election of a Labour government committed to that goal as part of a more 'ethical' foreign policy.

The question is how much of an arms industry will Britain retain at the start of the next millennium to meet these problems either by exports or by sales to the Ministry of Defence? The answer to the question will have a major impact not merely upon British defence preparedness but also upon the effective conduct of foreign policy.

The Past

During the Cold War arms transfers from one state to another were an important foreign policy tool of the Super Powers and their allies. They were used to befriend uncommitted states, to cement alliances and to assist states engaged in conflicts where the Super Powers could not risk committing their own forces. Towards the end of the Cold War, when the Soviets had lost their ideological magnetism and been left far behind economically by the West and the Asian Tigers, arms transfers were one of the very few ways that Moscow could still assert its Super Power status and cement links with friendly states in the Third World.

In such circumstances attempts by President Carter and others to negotiate limits on arms transfers were doomed to failure and frustration. But, with the collapse of the Soviet Empire and the end of the Cold War, arms transfer limitations have returned to the international agenda.¹ As the result of some high-profile campaigns, international pressure has focused on particular weapons, notably anti-personnel mines, and a convention banning their use, production, transfer and stockpiling was opened for signature on 3 December 1997. The UN established a voluntary arms trade register in 1992 under which states can report their imports and exports of weaponry. Twenty-eight of the arms exporting countries also agreed in 1995 to co-operate together to control exports of weapons and of equipment which could have both civilian and military uses. But these measures are evidently not enough to satisfy a range of critics that the arms trade is under proper control.

The British Labour Government elected in 1997 has said that it will follow a high-minded foreign policy and committed itself to moving away from the allegedly too realistic policy of its predecessor. It is committed to creating a 'transparent and accountable' system of arms export licences. The new Foreign Secretary, Robin Cook, was shadow Trade and Industry Secretary during the 'arms for Iraq inquiry' and led the attack on the Conservative Government over the issue. As a sign of the new policy, the Labour Government vetoed the sale of six armoured Land Rovers to Indonesia under guidelines restricting the sale of weapons which can be used for internal repression. It is also pushing the European Union to establish rules for arms exports so that no member state will take advantage of the restraints exercised by another.²

This new policy is partly a response to intense pressure group activity. There is also evidence of heightened public sensitivity about such issues following the highly publicised role of the late

---

[1] On the arms trade see Basil Collier, *Arms and the Men*, London: Hamish Hamilton, 1980; Edward Kolodziej, *Making and Marketing Arms*, Princeton, 1987; David Mussington, *Understanding Contemporary Arms Transfers*, IISS Adelphi Paper, No. 291, 1994; Paul Cornish, *The Arms Trade and Europe*, Royal Institute of International Affairs, 1995; Paul Cornish, *Controlling the Contemporary Arms Trade*, London: Bowerdean, 1996.

[2] 'Cook accuses ministers of cover-up over defence exports to Baghdad', *The Times*, 12 November 1992; 'Cook halts export of armoured carriers', *The Times*, 27 September 1997; see also *The Labour Manifesto 1997*, section on arms control, and 'Britain to press EU for code on arms exports', *The Times*, 2 January 1998.

Princess of Wales in the campaign against the production and use of land mines. Moreover, the media now report directly and instantly from the dictatorships of the Third World and from the battlefields of Rwanda, Bosnia and Afghanistan. Television coverage makes their reports much more vivid and immediate for the mass of people than straightforward newspaper accounts used to be. While our predecessors had to use their imaginations, we know only too clearly what the destruction of a town or the massacre of an ethnic grouping looks like. There are a few conflicts, such as the war in East Timor between the Indonesian government and Fretilin guerrillas fighting for independence, which Western journalists find it difficult to cover. Western publics consequently understand the cycle of violence between the government and guerrilla forces, and the reprisals which this form of warfare often brings down on the heads of innocent civilians.[3] Some blame the weapons as much as the government and guerrillas involved for the scale of such disasters.

One consequence of the end of the Cold War is bound to be the development of a Western public more questioning than previously about the need for defence and for maintaining industries to produce weapons. After the Falklands, the Gulf War and peace keeping in Bosnia, the British armed forces are generally held in high repute and particular British weapons, such as the Harrier or Tornado, are familiar to millions. Junior and middle level servicemen have succeeded admirably in relating their experiences to television interviewers. It is the cost of the services which is questioned. The situation is very different in Russia, for example, where the armed forces themselves are discredited. A poll of 1,000 Russian high school children in the Autumn of 1997 showed that only 1 per cent regarded the military as a reputable profession, far below the Mafia or prostitution![4]

If defence capabilities are not to be seriously eroded, however, the public needs a more informed understanding of the role that the defence industry plays in supporting the armed forces and of

---

[3] Human rights groups claim that 200,000 have been killed in East Timor between 1975 and 1989. (See *SIPRI Yearbook*, 1990, p.406.)

[4] 'Russia putting profits before honour', *The Times*, 24 October 1997.

the vital contribution of arms exports to the industry's profitability. There is presently a real danger that a purely emotional response to the subject will destroy thousands of jobs and weaken Britain's ability to deal with future security threats, without contributing to the safety of those who have the misfortune to live in the regions swept by war.

The End of the Cold War

During the half century after the destruction of Nazism, defence budgets consumed a larger proportion of the national income than they had done in the long peace during the 19th century or during the short, uneasy peace between the two World Wars. If British defence expenditure amounted to 100 in 1900, by 1933 it had fallen to 42. It rose again to 230 in 1952, levelling off at 209 in 1955.[5] Force levels in NATO and the Warsaw Pact peaked in the mid-1950s with 760,000 British men and women serving in the armed forces, 785,000 Frenchmen, 4·5 million Soviets and 2·85 million Americans.[6] Together the British and French then had 1·54 million servicemen, which is more than the 1·36 million Americans or 1·24 million Russians under arms today. During the Cold War generations of expensive and complex weapons were produced, came into service and were scrapped on becoming obsolete, often without being used in violent conflict at all. If they were used in war, it was in situations far removed from those for which they were designed. Ships and aircraft designed to fight the Soviet Union deterred the Indonesians in the jungles of South East Asia in the 1960s or waged war against the Argentines in the South Atlantic two decades later. Challenger tanks intended for the North German plains fought against the Iraqis in the baking deserts of Kuwait in 1991.

Such weapons justified their costs both by the rôle which they actually played in wars against dictators in the Third World and by the perceived need to deter Soviet aggression in Europe. Heavy expenditure could not be avoided by arms control agreements between East and West because not a single treaty

---

[5] Alan Peacock and Jack Wiseman, *The Growth of Public Expenditure in the United Kingdom*, London: George Allen and Unwin, 1968, p. 170.

[6] *IISS Military Balance 1977/8*, p. 87.

was negotiated on conventional armaments, despite decades of negotiation during the Cold War years.[7] Even so, British defence expenditure gradually fell as a percentage of GDP. In 1950 defence and war-related expenditures consumed £1,030 million a year or between one-quarter and one-fifth of government spending of £4,539 million. By 1981 defence had fallen to 10·8 per cent of government spending; after the end of the Cold War it dropped to 8·9 per cent, which was below expenditure on education and health, while social security was consuming four times as much as defence or 34·2 per cent of government spending in 1993.[8]

Now that the Soviet Empire has disappeared, nearly all developed countries have cut their defence budgets. The previous British government spent £17,782 million on defence in 1992-93 and planned to cut this to £16,220 million or 2·7 per cent of GDP by 1998-99.[9] Service personnel numbered 327,100 in 1985 and 292,839 in 1992-93. They were to be reduced to 216,400 by 1998-99. The United States cut the number of its active divisions between 1990 and 1998 from 18 to 10, its aircraft carriers from 15 to 11, its major warships from 287 to 166, its ICBMs from 1,000 to 500 and its bombers from 324 to 92. The collapse in Russian power has been far greater than the controlled reductions in Britain and United States or than the decline in numbers of Russian servicemen would suggest. Nevertheless, the International Institute for Strategic Studies (IISS) estimates that Russia has cut annual tank production from 1,600 to 5, the number of infantry fighting vehicles produced annually from 3,400 to 250, of fighters and ground attack aircraft from 430 to 25 and the number of ICBMs and SLBMs constructed from 115 to 10. In December 1997 President Yeltsin proposed further cuts of one-third in the number of Russian nuclear warheads in

---

[7] Philip Towle, *Arms Control and East-West Relations*, Beckenham, Kent: Croom Helm, 1983.

[8] For government expenditure in 1950 see Peacock and Wiseman, *op.cit.*, p.55; for 1993, see *Social Trends 1995 Edition*, London: Government Statistical Service, p. 112.

[9] *Statement on Defence Estimates, 1996*, Cm. 3223, p.51.

Table 1: Defence Expenditure[10]

in Constant 1995 US Dollars (millions)

	1985	1996
Germany	48,149	38,432
Britain	43,536	32,764
France	44,604	46,217
USA	352,551	265,823

in Per Capita US Dollars

	1985	1996
Germany	634	474
Britain	770	561
France	808	792
USA	1,473	1,001

as a Percentage of GDP

	1985	1996
Germany	3·2	1·7
Britain	5·2	3·0
France	4·0	3·1
USA	6·5	3·6

service and 40 per cent in force levels.[11] Meanwhile, the Russians are restructuring their forces and redirecting spending to new generations of advanced high-tech weapons, despite daunting economic and political problems.

Nevertheless, such reductions are so dramatic that they have to be compared to the disarmament which took place after the World Wars ended in 1815, 1918 and 1945. The so-called 'peace dividend' may not have been obvious immediately after the Cold War but it has gradually emerged nonetheless (see Table 1).

---

[10] *IISS Military Balance 1996/7*, p.306, and *1997/8*, p. 292.

[11] For Russian production figures see *IISS Military Balance 1996/7*, p. 110. See also 'Yeltsin cutting nuclear warheads by third', *The Times*, 3 December 1997, and 'Yelstin arms cut catches military aides off guard', *The Times*, 4 December 1997.

The Impact on Arms Manufacturing

As defence budgets have fallen so, inevitably, procurement has been cut. Some equipment has been cancelled altogether, other weapons deliveries have been spread over a longer period. Arms deliveries from one NATO or West European state to another were worth $15,142 million in 1987 and $8,635 million in 1995. Arms manufacturers have responded to the end of the Cold War by closing plants, by amalgamating and by searching for export markets. Conversion of arms-making factories to civilian uses has been tried but has rarely been successful. In the USA, Lockheed has combined with Martin, Northrop with Grumman and Boeing with McDonnell Douglas. At the same time the Stockholm International Peace Research Institute (SIPRI) has estimated that the number of employees in US military aircraft, missiles and space industries has fallen from 627,000 to 326,000.[12] In 1994 the British government reported that defence spending and exports supported 560,000 jobs in manufacturing; by 1996 this had fallen to 400,000, with between one-third and a half depending on exports.[13]

Britain holds a much larger share of the market in weapons exports than it maintains in most other areas of industrial production. In 1996 the government calculated that this amounted to about 20 per cent of world markets. For most other industrial products, the British share had fallen well below this level many years before. Steel exports fell from over 10 per cent to under 10 per cent between 1955 and 1965, car exports from under 30 per cent to under 20 per cent during the same period, textiles and electrical machinery from over 20 per cent to just over 10 per cent in the same decade. The total British share of world manufacturing exports fell from 20 per cent to nearer 10 per cent during that period and has continued to fall subsequently. In 1950 British exports were nearly as large as those from the Federal Republic of Germany (FRG) and France

---

[12] *SIPRI Yearbook 1996*, p.421.

[13] *Statement on Defence Estimates 1994*, Cm. 2550, p. 66; *Statement on Defence Estimates 1996*, Cm. 3223, p. 51.

Table 2: Arms Imports in Constant 1995 US Dollars (million)

	1987	1995
NATO and W. Europe	15,142	8,635
Latin America	5,100	1,540
Sub-Saharan Africa	6,511	300
Australasia	1,236	960
South Asia	6,291	1,330
Middle East and North Africa	31,862	14,385

combined, but by 1960 the FRG alone had overtaken Britain, and France was not far behind.[14]

Today foreign markets have become ever more competitive and the end of the Cold War has made the arms market particularly difficult. Although the market for weapons within NATO and Western Europe has fallen by almost a half in real terms, as a percentage of the world trade in arms it grew from 17.8 per cent to 22 per cent between 1987 and 1996. In part this is because the market within Eastern Europe has collapsed from 8.1 per cent of the world trade in arms to 3.1 per cent over the same period. Markets in South Asia, Latin America, Sub-Saharan Africa and Australasia have also shrunk in real terms (Table 2).[15]

It is sometimes suggested that reductions in weapons imports in most parts of the world have been accompanied by a rise in the East Asian arms market. Certainly its relative importance has grown but sales to East Asia have still fallen from $10,071 million to $8,535 million over the same period. Although the IISS detected a reversal of the general decline and growth of 8 per cent in real terms in the world arms trade in 1996, this trend will be stopped following the devastating Asian currency turmoil during the winter of 1997-98.[16]

---

[14] M. Blackwell, *Post War Europe, A Political Geography*, London: Hutchinson, 1981, p.44. See also 'UK share in world export manufactures', *Sunday Times*, 24 September 1967.

[15] *IISS Military Balance 1997/8*, p. 265.

[16] *IISS Military Balance 1997/8*, p. 264.

The Nature of Conflict After the Cold War

Commentators frequently suggest that the shape of conflict has changed since the end of the Cold War and that there has been a rise in the proportion of civil and guerrilla wars. There is no evidence for this in the world as a whole, though it is true that some regions which were kept free of conflict by the Soviet forces, such as Eastern Europe and the Caucasus, have been riven by disputes after the collapse of the Soviet Empire. Thus the civil strife which has devastated large parts of Asia and Africa since they achieved independence, has now spread to Eastern Europe as well. Although there have been about a dozen major inter-state wars since the Second World War (the Korean War, the various Arab-Israeli and Indo-Pakistan Wars, the Iran-Iraq War, the Falklands War and the Gulf War), the vast majority of conflicts have taken place within states.[17] There has been no change in this respect since the end of the Cold War.

Immediately after the Second World War most conflicts took the form of anti-colonial struggles as the British, French, Dutch and others strove to hold on to their colonial empires. With the failure of these efforts, more than a hundred new and weak states emerged on the international scene. Their civil services were often rudimentary, their armed forces mutinous and arrogant, and their politicians ineffective and corrupt. With the legitimacy of their governmental institutions in question, many of the new states have subsequently been the scene of civil wars, ethnic and religious rivalries, or insurgency. The development of Peoples' Wars from Maoist principles has introduced a new and devastating form of conflict on to the world stage. Considerable areas of the world, including Zaire, Rwanda, Somalia, Angola and Afghanistan, can barely be said to be states in the normal meaning of the term since the government, if there is one, has little control over large areas of 'its' territory and certainly no monopoly of the legitimate use of force. Some areas, such as Sri Lanka, while recognisably states, have been devastated by years of conflict, while yet others have been reduced to beggary by

---

[17] Some estimates give a much larger number of international conflicts but these include every skirmish: see Herbert K. Tillema, *International Armed Conflict since 1945*, Boulder: Westview Press, 1991.

decades of incompetent and rapacious government. Thus Haiti, which was ruled for many years by the corrupt and violent Duvalier family, had a GDP of $1,000 per head in 1996 against $4,300 in the Dominican Republic, which occupies the other half of the same island and which has had less incompetent rulers.[18]

It is in the context of the violence in these areas that arms sales policy has to be mainly considered. That is not to say that interstate conflict may not occur over the next 20 years on a major scale, particularly in East Asia. Recent tensions in the Korean peninsula or between China and Taiwan and between South Korea and Japan have reminded the world community of the potentially explosive nature of the territorial and other disputes in the Pacific region. These conflicts may be tempered and war avoided by the US military presence in the Pacific; it was US diplomats who negotiated the agreement with North Korea in 1994 to dissuade it from acquiring nuclear weapons, and it was the US which deterred Chinese intervention in Taiwanese affairs by sending its aircraft carriers to the region.[19] On the other hand, intra-state conflict in Africa, South Asia, the Caucasus and the Balkans is certain to continue. It is the impact of arms sales on potential international wars in the Pacific, South Asia and the Middle East, and on the intra-state wars elsewhere which has to be examined.

There are four main grounds on which arms sales have been criticised:

- *first*, that they can strengthen repressive régimes;

- *second*, that they may precipitate inter-state wars if they strengthen revisionist states;

- *third*, that they increase the number of casualties, particularly in civil and guerrilla wars; and,

- *fourth*, that they waste resources of poor states which should concentrate on developing their economy and infrastructure.

---

[18] *IISS Military Balance 1997/8*, pp.215 and 220.

[19] On the Korean nuclear deal see Philip Towle, *Enforced Disarmament*, Oxford: Clarendon Press, 1997, p. 202 *passim*.

Arms Sales and Government Repression

There would probably be majority support for a prohibition of arms exports which can help governments repress their populations, unless there are vital strategic reasons for supporting such régimes for a limited period. Fortunately, the dilemma is less pervasive as the number of military dictatorships has declined in Latin America and in East Asia. Military sales to Brazil or South Korea are therefore less controversial than they were 20 years ago. But the general problem is still to decide which régimes are repressive and which sort of weapons, if any, should be sold to the remaining dictatorships.

Some argue in principle that no arms should be sold to such governments, even weapons which cannot normally be used for internal repression, such as warships, air defence radars and anti-aircraft missiles. In practice, paradoxical as it may seem, it is the cheaper and simpler arms which are normally used to threaten the liberty of the citizen. It did not take tanks, aircraft or warships for the military junta in Argentina to kill up to 20,000 people during the 'dirty war' of the 1970s. The great massacres of the 20th century, of Armenians in Turkey during the First World War, of Kulaks in the Soviet Union, of Jews in Nazi Germany and of educated Cambodians in the 1970s, were all perpetrated with simple weapons. Small arms are the most effective instruments of repression. The case for restricting their sale is therefore stronger than is the case for banning the export of more sophisticated weapons; it should be borne in mind, however, that such bans, if effective, may only encourage indigenous arms production of the proscribed items. Major importers of armaments may respond to the restrictions by acquiring the capacity to develop even relatively sophisticated weapons, as South Africa did during the 1970s, but this can obviously be achieved more quickly and easily in the case of small arms.

If one can distinguish between the effects of different types of weapons, so one can distinguish between different types of non-democratic régimes. Are traditional monarchies naturally repressive? The question is of importance since Saudi Arabia and the Gulf states have been major importers of Western weapons over the last 20 years. Saudi Arabia was the third largest importer between 1991 and 1995, Kuwait was the 12th and the United

Arab Emirates the 24th.[20] However, the Gulf monarchies are not like the (former) African dictators, such as Amin of Uganda or Mobutu of Zaire, because they have a coherent Moslem philosophy, the legitimacy which their history allows, and a very considerable reservoir of admiration and sympathy amongst the traditionally minded members of their own communities. The monarchs do not observe Western constitutional and legal niceties. They may eventually be overthrown, as the kings were in Egypt, Libya, Iran and Iraq but, in the meantime, the West cannot impose its values on these states and it has a major interest in the stability of the Gulf region, because of its oil reserves. It is not, therefore, surprising or unreasonable that Western governments have often responded to the Gulf rulers' anxieties about security by supplying the arms they request.

Apart from sales to the Gulf states, it is arms exports to Indonesia which have caused most anxiety in Britain in recent years. In particular it was the export of Hawk aircraft to Indonesia which aroused most debate. With nearly 200 million people and an economic growth rate of 8.2 per cent in 1995 and 7.8 per cent the following year, Indonesia was clearly an important market before the recent Asian currency turmoil. It is the largest Moslem state and a regional power of some significance.

Critics of the Hawk deal argued that General Suharto's government was brutal and dictatorial. Even though Djakarta promised not to use the Hawks against the guerrillas in East Timor, many felt that its word could not be trusted. Certainly aircraft of the Hawk type can be used against insurgents, though their high speed makes them less effective than helicopters in this role. What are needed by the government are very slow aircraft which can be used to locate and track small bands of insurgents even in broken terrain and jungle. Moreover, civilian helicopters can be easily bought on the international market or manufactured locally and converted into much more effective anti-insurgent weapons than Hawks. To put it another way, assuming a fixed defence budget, the more the Indonesians spend on Hawks the

---

[20] *SIPRI Yearbook, 1996*, p. 466.

less money they have to spend on dedicated anti-insurgent aircraft.[21]

The size of the Indonesian market, the importance of the deal to British Aerospace, the promise that the aircraft would not be used in East Timor and the fact that more deadly weapons could be bought so easily, persuaded previous British governments to go ahead with the deal despite very reasonable anxieties about East Timor. As so often with arms deals, the issue is less clearcut than those who cry for a purely 'moral' policy usually allow. Debate on this subject needs to be tempered by a recognition that civil order is a necessary, if not sufficient, condition of economic and political progress. Outside East Timor, Indonesia has been a better place to live over the last decade than Rwanda, Somalia, or Afghanistan. South Korea and Taiwan, authoritarian states only a decade ago, have become wealthy democracies. The road to peace and prosperity in collapsed states is going to be very much harder. If imperfect leaders in the Third World are to be censured and denied the means to maintain power, we must be very confident that their likely successors prove to be more enlightened, or we will be in danger of putting the purity of our own motives before the well-being of those for whom we affect concern.

Arms Sales and Inter-State Conflicts

As the arms trade's critics have always maintained, there have been several cases in recent years where arms sales have encouraged the outbreak of war. Very large Soviet exports of arms to Somalia in the 1970s fuelled Somali irredentism towards Ethiopia and Kenya. Between 1973 and 1974 alone the Soviets allegedly supplied 120 aircraft, including helicopters, fighters and transports.[22] During its struggle against Iran in the 1980s, Iraq bought armoured cars from Brazil, main battle tanks from China, helicopters and missiles from France, frigates and corvettes from Italy, tanks, artillery and Scud missiles from the USSR. According to SIPRI, Iraq was the leading arms importer

---

[21] Philip Towle, *Pilots and Rebels, The Use of Aircraft in Unconventional Warfare*, London: Brassey's, 1989, Chapter Four.

[22] *SIPRI Yearbook, 1996*, p. 466.

in the Third World in 1983, 1984 and 1985. Over the years between 1983 and 1987 Baghdad imported $15,736 million worth of equipment, its only Third World rival being India with $12,589 million in imports.[23] By 1988-89 Iraq had over one million men in its armed forces, 5,500 main battle tanks (at a time when Britain had 1,200), 3,000 towed artillery, 160 armed helicopters, 70 MiG 23, 64 Mirage F1 and 25 MiG 25 fighters.[24]

After the end of the Iran-Iraq War, these imports left Baghdad deeply in debt to its Arab neighbours and encouraged Saddam Hussein to try to solve his economic problems by seizing one of his largest creditors, the Emirate of Kuwait. US resolve to resist his aggression precipitated the 1991 Gulf War.[25]

But arms transfers can be stabilising. To make what should be an obvious point, what matters crucially is who has the weapons and for what purpose. Supplies to status quo powers can discourage attacks by revisionist states. Britain rushed supplies to Kenya in the 1970s when the eccentric and brutal ruler of Uganda, Idi Amin, threatened Nairobi. Washington has tried over the last three decades to keep Israeli weaponry at a level which would discourage Arab revisionism, whilst simultaneously encouraging the Israelis to negotiate a lasting settlement of the Palestinian problem. Such activities can, of course, go badly wrong if they are misjudged. Paris and Moscow could justify their supplies to Iraq in the 1980s on the grounds that otherwise the Iranians would emerge victorious from the war and spread their brand of Moslem fundamentalism through the oil-bearing regions of the Middle East. Nor were these pleas entirely without foundation. Left to themselves, 69 million Iranians, many with a fanatical belief in their revolutionary Moslem government, would have defeated Iraq with only one-third the number of people. The arms exporters, led by France and the USSR, needed to be able to supply Iraq with just enough weapons to keep Iran at bay without encouraging its expansionism in other directions. If they were genuinely searching for such a middle way, they failed to

---

[23] *SIPRI Yearbook*, 1988, p. 179.

[24] *IISS Military Balance 1988*, p. 101.

[25] Roland Dannreuther, *The Gulf Conflict, A Political and Strategic Analysis*, IISS Adelphi Paper No. 264, Winter 1981/2.

discover it, though they could still argue that the Gulf War was less disastrous than an Iranian victory would have been because of the threat which Iran's Moslem ideology represented to the rest of the Middle East.

During the Cold War the two Super Powers preferred to supply arms to allied and friendly states rather than to become directly involved in conflicts. They could not risk the possibility that they would both be drawn in on opposite sides to some regional war and that this would lead to a conflict between NATO and the Warsaw Pact. The most spectacular example of this strategy was the Arab-Israeli War of 1973. The surprise Arab attack on Israel enabled the Egyptians with their Soviet-supplied equipment to establish their forces across the Suez Canal, whilst the Syrians almost broke through Israeli defences in the north. Israeli air power, which had dominated the 1967 Arab-Israeli War, was to some extent negated by the power of the Egyptian missile defences. The balance was changed by the sudden flood of US aircraft and other equipment which enabled the Israelis to recover their position. Had this not been possible, the United States might have been drawn directly into the conflict or the Israelis might have resorted to the use of nuclear weapons.[26]

Since the end of the Cold War there has been less need for Washington to avoid direct involvement in conflicts because the threat of a confrontation with Moscow has been so much reduced. Nevertheless, there may be circumstances where it will not want to become embroiled in a war, while still wanting to support a friendly country such as Israel or Taiwan. Severe restrictions on arms transfers would circumscribe its ability to do so or make its government resort to covert means of support. There is evidence that the USA supplied the Bosnian government with weapons during the early 1990s in defiance of the UN arms embargo.[27]

All this means that arms transfers can be either stabilising or destabilising. But while 'arms races' between states may serve

---

[26] For the 1973 war see A.B. Adan, *The Banks of Suez*, London: Arms and Armour Press, 1980; Chaim Herzog, *The Arab Israeli Wars*, London: Arms and Armour Press, 1982.

[27] David Owen, *Balkan Odyssey*, London: Victor Gollancz, 1995, p.356.

as barometers of underlying political conflicts, may exacerbate tensions, may even decide the timing of a decision to go to war, the ultimate, underlying causes are always political.

In reality, the effect of arms sales depends upon the quality of the political judgements of the governments in the exporting states, which is why Britain, in common with most Western states, has a system of export licences. They may be tempted for purely economic gains to resort to arms exports, even to régimes known to be expansionist, but the potential losses in both economic and human terms should give them pause. With the destruction they bring, wars deepen hostilities, waste resources and make permanent settlements more difficult.

Arms Sales and Casualties

Contrary to the views expressed in what is becoming a very one-sided debate, there is no correlation between the cost of weapons imports into a particular region and the prevalence of warfare there. Sub-Saharan Africa has been the region most devastated by war over the last decade yet, as we have seen, arms sales to the region have shrunk dramatically in dollar terms. Afghanistan has continued to be torn apart by wars, yet the statistics suggest that military expenditure there fell from $392 million in 1987 to $200 million in 1996.[28] However, these figures ignore smuggling and particularly the steady flow of cheap Kalashnikov rifles to these regions. In these bitter internecine wars the combatants buy the weapons which are most effective, not those which appeal to national prestige or impress foreign visitors.

Most casualties in the intra-state wars which have swept the post-colonial world have been caused by small arms, anti-personnel mines and artillery. Very few have been the result of the use of tanks, aircraft and other sophisticated weaponry. Thus the deals which are listed on the UN Register and those which most benefit the arms makers are the ones which had little or no role in the bloodshed in the Third World. Unfortunately, the large deals are also those which governments can best control, while

---

[28] *IISS Military Balance 1997/8*, p. 150.

the small arms and anti-personnel mines, which are so destructive, have largely escaped observation and control.[29]

There are certain types of weapons which could change this picture and greatly increase the casualty rate in wars within the Third World. In the 1970s the Soviets began to export Scud and other missiles to Afghanistan, North Korea and Iran. These had been primarily designed to carry nuclear warheads and they were too inaccurate to be effective against precise military targets with high explosive warheads. The temptation for importers was to use them against cities and to try to adapt them to carry chemical and biological warheads. The developed countries have responded to these dangers by establishing the Missile Technology Control Regime to inhibit further sales of such weapons. However, North Korea and other states outside the Regime, which have some ability to manufacture missiles, reduce its efficacy. There are now treaties banning the production both of chemical and of biological weapons but again the problems arise from those countries which are not parties and which may be working on such weapons of mass destruction.

Arms Deals and Third World Resources

Any resources spent on defence can be criticised for taking money away from other public benefits, such as health and education. These criticisms are particularly telling when large areas of the Third World are ravaged by disease and when illiteracy continues to be so widespread. However, many of the states, which have expended substantial resources on weapons imports over recent decades, have not been poor and backward. Saudi Arabia had a *per capita* GDP of $10,200 in 1996, half as much as the British level but twice the level of Turkey. Kuwait had a GDP of $16,200, more than Spain, Portugal or Greece. The East Asian importers, such as Japan, South Korea and Taiwan, have also been relatively wealthy. The South Korean GDP per head in 1996 was $12,400, Japan's was $23,200 and Taiwan's

---

[29] For one recent look at the problem see J. Singh (ed.), *Light Weapons and International Security*, Pugwash and Basic, December 1995.

$11,700. Selling weapons to such countries is no different in economic terms from selling any other consumer goods.[30] At one time the idea was prevalent that high defence expenditure and rapid economic growth were mutually exclusive.[31] Japan and the FRG were the strongest and fastest growing economies, and also had low levels of defence spending. But this belief in the retarding effect of defence spending became much less fashionable in the 1980s after the Asian Tigers took over from Japan and the FRG as the most rapidly growing economies. South Korea grew by 9 per cent in 1995 and 7.1 per cent in 1996, yet it had 672,000 men in its armed forces, and mobilised 2,130 main battle tanks and 461 combat aircraft. Taiwan mobilised 376,000 men and maintained reserves of 1.65 million out of a population of 21 million, yet it has become one of the most dynamic and successful economies in the world.[32]

Of course it is true that some of the much poorer states have also imported considerable numbers of weapons from the West. India had a per capita GDP of only $1,500 in 1996, yet for much of the 1980s it was one of the largest Third World importers of sophisticated weapons. It has an aircraft carrier equipped with Sea Harriers, an air force armed with MiG 23, MiG 27 and Jaguar aircraft, and its army of just under a million men has about 3,300 main battle tanks. Pakistan is slightly wealthier with a GDP per head of $2,300 dollars but it has also armed heavily against its neighbour with 2,120 mainly Chinese-made tanks and 429 combat aircraft.[33] Critics would suggest that Western, Soviet and Chinese supplies have fed the Indo-Pakistan arms race and accentuated divisions in the sub-continent. On their side the Indian and Pakistani governments have argued vociferously against any limitations on arms exports which they maintain are motivated by neo-colonialism and racist assumptions about their

---

[30] *IISS Military Balance 1997/8*, section on East Asia and Australasia, p. 164 *passim*.

[31] L. Freedman, *Arms Production in the United Kingdom, Problems and Prospects*, London: Royal Institute of International Affairs, 1978, discusses this assessment.

[32] *IISS Military Balance 1997/8*, pp. 184 and 193.

[33] *IISS Military Balance 1997/8*, pp. 153 and 159. On Indian defence policy see Damon Bristow, *India's New Armament Strategy: A Return to Self-Sufficiency?*, London: Royal United Services Institute for Defence Studies, 1995.

unfitness to be trusted with advanced weaponry. Clearly, defence expenditure has been a heavy burden on the two states, with Pakistan spending over 7 per cent of its GNP on its armed forces through much of the 1970s. Equally clearly, it is not the primary reason for Indo-Pakistan hostility or for the poverty of the subcontinent. As in the Arab-Israeli dispute, only a diplomatic solution to the long-standing regional conflict over Kashmir will undermine the demand for weaponry.[34]

The Response from Defence Industries

Defence industries were frequently criticised during the Cold War years, particularly for their role in supplying weapons to the Third World. But they knew that governments would protect them because of their vital contribution to the West's defences. Such protection may continue but it will be weaker after the Cold War. More needs to be done to demonstrate that they are not responsible for the conditions of countries torn by war.

Exporters need to retain as much control as possible over the weapons they manufacture and transfer to other countries. High technology equipment, such as aircraft and missiles, very quickly becomes unserviceable if spares are not available and those spares can usually only come from the original manufacturer. The problem, as we have seen, is that it is low technology which is responsible for most deaths and governmental repression in the Third World – anti-personnel mines, infantry weapons and artillery. Certain anti-personnel mines have already been developed to become ineffective or destroy themselves after a set time. The principle of controlled degradation needs extending wherever possible to infantry and artillery weapons.

There would indeed be something to be said for banning exports of small arms altogether, except to the armed forces of Western democratic states. This would dissociate the United Kingdom from the most destructive aspect of the arms trade. The profits Britain makes from this trade are very small, though such a proscription would badly damage certain specialised makers who sell very small numbers of hand-built rifles to wealthy

---

[34] For a recent analysis of the Indo-Pakistan problem see Maroff Raza, *Wars and No Peace over Kashmir*, New Delhi: Lancer Publishing, 1996.

foreigners for sporting purposes. The other larger group damaged would be companies which sell second-hand weapons to the Third World.[35] Some would also argue that such a self-denying ordinance by Britain would have no impact whatsoever either on the magnitude of the trade in small arms or on the dozens of intra-state wars currently occurring in Africa, Central Asia and elsewhere because few countries would follow Britain's lead. Any reduction in the world-wide supply of such weapons would lead to an increase in their price, and thus provide an incentive to alternative suppliers.[36]

The collapse of the Soviet Union precipitated a flood of small arms across the world and members of the armed and security forces, or former members, are deeply implicated in the export of weapons of all types.[37] Many other Western states allow large quantities of weapons to remain in the hands of hunters and others with legitimate sporting interest in weaponry. Governments will be rightly reluctant to offend such groups by imposing severe restrictions.

Nevertheless, the argument that others will export weapons, even if Britain desists, is a dangerous defence for any aspect of the arms trade. The very same argument was used to defend the slave trade in the 18th century and the opium trade to China in the 19th century.[38] If that is the main argument in favour of such exports, the public may say that the sacrifice is worth making and turn on small arms exports in the same way that they have turned on the suppliers of anti-personnel mines. In this case also one could argue that self-denying prohibitions by the developed states will have relatively little effect on the conflicts in the Third World because anti-personnel mines can so easily be manufactured in the zones of conflict themselves. Yet most Western states will adhere to the prohibition on anti-personnel

---

[35] G. Thayer, *The War Business*, London: Weidenfeld and Nicolson, 1969, Part Two.

[36] Bernard Levin, 'A gun in every hand', *The Times*, 28 June 1991; John Grigg, 'The issues the headlines hid', *The Times*, 28 December 1991; 'Gun culture delivers record murder rates', *The Times*, 30 December 1993.

[37] 'Ex KGB agents ply trade in weapons', *The Times*, 21 September 1993.

[38] For the debate on opium see *Hansard Parliamentary Debates*, Third Series, 31 July 1843 to 24 August 1843, p. 241 *passim*.

mines. Moreover, self-interest should make the West more anxious about rifles than about mines. Anti-personnel mines are not a threat to the Western states themselves because they are unlikely to be smuggled into their territory and used for robbery and murder. The spread of handguns across the Third World is a serious threat because they fall into the hands of criminals even in law-abiding states such as Britain.[39]

Conclusion

The export of expensive and advanced weaponry, such as aircraft, warships and tanks, is not akin to the slave trade from Africa to the Americas, as one writer claimed recently, nor is it akin to the 19th-century drugs trade with China.[40] Carefully controlled by astute governments, arms exports can deter wars between Third World states and they can distance the Great Powers from conflicts in which they do not wish to become directly involved.

Exports of new or second-hand small arms are much more difficult to defend. They are not effective deterrents of war between one state and another. Although they have their legitimate uses even by authoritarian régimes they can also be used for purposes of repression and by xenophobic nationalists to attack other ethnic groups. They are an important contributor to the erosion of control by governments and thus the spread of anarchy across large swathes of the world. They are used by those responsible for the great majority of deaths in violent conflict in the Third World. They usually escape from the control of the manufacturer as soon as they leave the factory door and they frequently fall into the hands of drug smugglers and other criminals. Their manufacture and sale produce few economic

---

[39] 'Condon warns of growing threat from illegal guns', *The Times*, 1 September 1994; 'Stop the hour of the gun before it starts', *Guardian*, 5 September 1995; 'Street fighting men', *Guardian*, 19 September 1995. The export of small arms is also causing increasing concern to the US government which believes that its European allies are too lax in their licensing procedure for re-exporting US manufactured weapons. See 'EU arms "loophole" comes under fire', *International Herald Tribune*, and 'Dispute grows over export of US guns', *The Times*, 20 April 1998.

[40] Linda Colley, review of *The Slave Trade* by Hugh Thomas, *The Times*, 27 November 1997.

benefits and they sully the rest of the arms trade with their effects.

Criticism of the arms trade has grown because of confusion between the different types of weapons and their impact. Governments have also often found it difficult to explain the reasons for exporting sophisticated weapons to particular countries. In some cases the importers do not want to offend neighbouring states by explaining their fears and the need for weapons. In other cases those who seek to represent Western public opinion dismiss these fears without really understanding them. It always seems easy to 'solve' a dispute half a world away.

Justifying arms sales is thus frequently difficult. It will be more difficult for this British government because of its commitment to a more 'ethical' foreign policy, and the activities of those seeking to push the government still further. Yet exports of sophisticated weapons to carefully chosen states can enhance stability and strengthen Britain's defence industrial base. In complex real-life situations ethical judgements require fine distinctions and difficult calculations; these seem largely absent from the blanket condemnations of arms exports. The irony of all this is that those in Whitehall and Westminster who wrestle with complex calculations as to the merits of alternative courses of actions when deciding whether to permit arms exports, come closer to meeting the criteria for moral judgement than do many critics of the present system.

Fifty years ago the world was rescued from the helotry and genocide of the Nazi and Japanese empires by aircraft, tanks and warships produced by British and US manufacturers.[41] We need to retain a substantial defence industry to face an uncertain future and, for that, arms exports have become even more essential with the contraction of Britain's own forces.

---

[41] For Nazi forms of helotry see Ulrich Herbert, *Hitler's Foreign Workers, Forced Labour in Germany under the Third Reich*, Cambridge: Cambridge University Press, 1997.